PREPARING LEADERS FOR FULL-SPECTRUM OPERATIONS

Introduction

The United States began this century with the world's preeminent conventional military force and validated this title with overwhelming battlefield victories against the Taliban and the Iraqi Military. Once again, the American military was able to overwhelm Iraqi conventional forces in a short time period with minimal American casualties. These successes seemed to validate the superiority of our equipment, doctrine, and the training and professional education of our military's leaders. However, soon after these euphoric battlefield victories the Army found itself ill prepared for stability operations in Iraq and an emerging insurgency.

General Keane addressed our shortcomings in irregular warfare as American Forces became consumed with a growing insurgency in Iraq. "We put an Army on the battlefield that I had been a part of for 37 years. It doesn't have any doctrine, nor was it educated and trained, to deal with an insurgency. After the Vietnam War we purged ourselves of everything that had to do with irregular warfare or insurgency, because it had to do with how we lost that war. In hindsight a bad decision." [1]

Army doctrine states that its forces must be able to dominate military conflict throughout the full spectrum of conflict. This injunction appears in the recently published Field Manual Army Operations (FM 3.0) but was also true in the last version published in 2001. The Army has always been expected to dominate militarily from stable peace through general war. What happened? Leading up to our military commitments in Iraq and Afghanistan, the Army was shaped by decades of preparing for, and executing, major conventional wars against its cold war adversaries. The legacy of the Cold War was aggravated by America's traditional aversion to protracted conflicts, distaste for irregular warfare, and especially counterinsurgency operations following the Vietnam experience, and the nature of our involvement in post-cold war conflicts prior to the attacks on September 11th, 2001.

The purpose of this paper is to examine the Army's recent and current training and education focus and provide recommendations addressing where and how the Army can best focus these programs in the future to ensure leaders are adequately prepared to operate effectively throughout the full spectrum of conflict. The Army was caught short in COIN proficiency as it began operations in Iraq and Afghanistan but has made dramatic strides in the past couple of years. Currently, the Army has published new COIN doctrine, adjusted training venues to emphasize COIN over conventional warfighting, and incorporated COIN into our officer and NCO education systems. This emphasis addresses many of the deficiencies the Army confronted in Iraq. But is this new focus compromising our ability to dominate future adversaries throughout the spectrum of conflict? Should the Army transition to our traditional preparation for major combat operations at the higher end of the spectrum of conflict?

Background

The United States Army began the 21st Century fixated on high intensity warfare which resulted in Army leaders being unprepared to effectively conduct COIN operations following the conventional fight in Iraq. While the Army had considerable experiences with Peace Operations, it was not prepared to combat an insurgency. The Army had no current COIN doctrine, had not trained for COIN, and COIN was not adequately addressed in its institutional education system. Most leaders lacked an understanding of the complexities of COIN operations and tended to focus on the threat or use of kinetic force to accomplish their objective of defeating the insurgency.

Post War Training and Education

The post Cold War Army recognized that future battlefields were going to be more complex and began adapting the Army's training and education programs to address likely scenarios in the future. The Army gained experiences in Peace Operations such as Somalia, Haiti, Bosnia, and Kosovo. The Army updated its operations doctrine in 1994 and again in 2001. The term "spectrum of conflict" in our previous capstone doctrine FM 3-0 Operations (2001) outlined the operations which the military must be prepared to execute at all times. While this doctrine addressed peace operations at the lower end of the spectrum, in hindsight insurgency was conspicuously absent.

The Army made changes to its training and education programs during the 1990s. Military Operations Other Than War (MOOTW) became an important topic driving the Army's focus on training and education. The idea that urbanization would increase the likelihood of combat operations in the midst of civilians became a major concern for the Army's leadership. This uneasiness resulted in the use of civilians on the battlefield (COBs) at the Combat Maneuver Training Center in Germany and the Joint Readiness Training Center at Fort Polk Louisiana. This training forced leaders and their soldiers to plan for the impact of civilians on their operations.

The use of COBs and inclusion of (MOOTW) training was beneficial to units given the frequent employment of American troops in Peace Support Operations throughout the 1990s. Units became more proficient exercising Rules of Engagement and considering the impact of civilians on the battlefield. However, it can argued that civilians were primarily viewed as an impediment to operations and many leaders focused on civilian casualty avoidance rather than attempting to communicate and build relationships with the local populace. Despite this increased complexity of training, counterinsurgency training was seldom addressed at the Army's training centers and was mostly absent from the curriculums of our NCO and officer professional development courses as the Army began to execute the Global War on Terrorism.

Necessary Adjustments Made

> The soldiers must then be prepared to serve as a propagandist, a social worker, a civil engineer, a school teacher, a nurse, a boy scout...Counterinsurgency is 20 percent combat and 80 percent political.[2]

The Army became bogged down in combating a stubborn and complex insurgency in Iraq and the Army recognized its deficiencies in COIN. The Army quickly adapted training and education courses to focus on counterinsurgency and cultural training to prepare units for their deployments in support of Operation Iraqi Freedom (OIF) and Operation Enduring Freedom (OEF). Beginning with OIF II, many units completed a Mission Readiness Exercise (MRX) providing them an opportunity to train in a counterinsurgency environment. Counterinsurgency was reemphasized in the Army's professional education programs and it is now the primary focus for individual and collective training.

The Army has made tremendous progress in rectifying shortcomings in COIN by adjusting its education systems and training programs. In fact, arguably these programs have now become COIN centric. The Army's educational systems and training venues quickly adjusted focus from major combat operations at the higher end of the spectrum of conflict to deal with an insurgency. Along with institutional changes, junior leaders are obtaining invaluable tactical and operational experiences in COIN as a result of multiple deployments in support of the Global War on Terror.

The professional education of commissioned and non-commissioned officers has radically changed since the start of the Global War on Terrorism. Counterinsurgency was mostly absent from curriculums of Non-Commissioned Officer's Courses, and the Captain's Career Course. Now all of these courses clearly emphasize counterinsurgency operations throughout their curriculum. [3] According to an official at the Command and General Staff College, Counterinsurgency has been heavily introduced into the curriculum.[4] In fact, the course work for the Intermediate Leadership Education Course at the Command and General Staff College has increased core course hours dedicated to counterinsurgency from 30 to 200. An additional 40 hours is available through electives.[5]

Most units focus almost exclusively on COIN training at home station and many conduct Mission Rehearsal Exercises (MRX) emphasizing COIN prior to deployment. The Combat Training Centers have become even more capable than ever in replicating conditions that leaders will likely experience in Iraq and Afghanistan. For example, the National Training Center has fully integrated a COIN capacity into their programs by integrating lessons learned, making physical changes to the NTC environment, and by developing a Full-Spectrum training environment that can realistically replicate a COIN environment.[6]

The National Training Center provides a realistic COIN environment with the ability to provide mission rehearsal exercises in support of training units including the development of a complex 1600 person role player capability. These role players include roughly 250 Iraqi Americans capable of playing the roles of tribal and religious leaders as well as replicating family, social, and business relationships. The Army has completed construction of 13 towns and villages in both live-fire and force on force environments, built Forward Operating Bases, and improved instrumentation including infrared and low light video cameras to aid in the collection of feedback.[7]

Noteworthy is the shift to intelligence driven operations and the ability to link unit actions with scenario outcomes supported by a software program called the Reactive Information Propaganda Planning for Life like Exercises (RIPPLE). This allows exercise designers to select the right actions to create credible cause and effect relationships.[8] This is a superb innovation to train leaders in adhering to the counterinsurgency principle of winning the fight for the support of the population.

The Army rapidly energized its efforts to rectify COIN deficiencies by publishing FM 3-24 Counterinsurgency Operations in 2006. Publication of this current doctrine, along with tailored predeployment training, and the incorporation of COIN into the Army's professional military education programs, has been instrumental in rebuilding the Army's competence in combating insurgencies. These radical efforts combined with the combat experiences gained by leaders and soldiers through multiple deployments and over four years of conducting COIN have clearly increased their competence in successfully operating against an insurgency.

However, these improvements resulted from a reaction to events. The Army's initial ignorance of insurgency and COIN principles may have significantly contributed to the growth of the insurgency in Iraq. Additionally, while American soldiers are now

6

battle hardened, they are losing their edge in fighting major conventional combat operations.

Consider that the Army's training centers are not currently hosting conventional rotations. For example, the National Training Center has not exercised a traditional training rotation for several years and there is limited or no high intensity conventional training being conducted. Further, maneuver training is mostly confined to company and platoon level.[9] This means that current company commanders have limited or no conventional experience in maneuvering units at the platoon level. Soon field grade officers will have no conventional maneuver experience what so ever.[10] Certainly investment in rethinking the Army's training and education programs must occur to ensure our leaders are prepared for future conflicts through proactive rather than reactive measures.

Secretary Robert M. Gates stated "One of the principal challenges the Army faces, is to regain its traditional edge at fighting conventional wars while retaining what it has learned- and unlearned about unconventional wars, the ones most likely to be fought in the years ahead."[11] The Army must address how it intends to balance preparations for future threats and must carefully consider whether it is prudent to focus efforts at either end of the spectrum. Likewise, it would be impossible to reach the highest competencies in every form of conflict simultaneously. There are fears that the current preoccupation with COIN is dominating leader development and is contributing to a decline in America's unrivaled competency in conventional warfighting.

There are several competing opinions concerning how the Army can best posture itself for future conflict. Some contend irregular warfare will be the dominate form of war in the future and that the risk of an adversary challenging our military with conventional capabilities is remote. They would argue that the Army should remain focused on training for irregular war and specifically counterinsurgency. Another option would be for the Army to reemphasize preparation for major combat operations at the higher end of the spectrum of conflict. A third option is for the Army to organize itself with COIN forces and traditional forces that focus their training at their respective ends of the spectrum of conflict. One would fight and win major conventional engagements, while the other would be adept at fighting insurgents and conducting stability operations. Finally, the Army could accept less expertise at either end of the spectrum of conflict by finding a balance in the education and training of its leaders.

Focus on Lower End of Conflict Such as COIN

Many believe that the risk of a major conventional war is remote in the foreseeable future. General Casey, Chief of Staff of the Army, stated "Folks aren't going to attack our strength, either in a regular war or conventional war. It's silly to". [12] The dominate opinion seems to be that irregular warfare and counterinsurgency will be the most common form of conflict that will challenge the American military in the 21st century. This is supported by the nature of our military commitments since the end of the Cold War. Our engagements in Panama, Haiti, Somalia, and currently Afghanistan and Iraq have clearly demonstrated the likelihood that irregular warfare is the dominate form of conflict. [13] The risk of the Army being involved in major combat operations is even more unlikely based on the dominate conventional capabilities of the U.S. military as demonstrated during Operation Desert Storm and more recently in the initial phases of Operation Enduring Freedom and Operation Iraqi Freedom. America's conventional forces quickly eliminated their adversaries' conventional capabilities to resist within days during all three conflicts.

The Army's lack of preparedness for mitigating the environmental conditions that fed an emerging insurgent movement had a considerable impact on the United States' role as the world's lone superpower. The international community has seen America's vulnerability to irregular warfare and the enormous commitment it has been required to make hindering its ability to project military power elsewhere. This vulnerability was demonstrated not only by our operations in Iraq and Afghanistan, but also by our experiences in Vietnam, Lebanon, and Somalia over the past four decades.[14] While potential adversaries may be surprised at America's will to remain committed in current operations, they have surely noted popular resentment of the conflict within the American people.

America's will to invest its blood and treasure in the future is tenuous at best, particularly when the justification for conflict is nebulous. Perhaps focusing on stability operations and irregular warfare would provide the Army with a decisive edge in future conflicts. The result when combined with the effective application of other instruments of power could shorten conflicts by competently mitigating conditions that support insurgencies and other sources of instability. Preparing for stability operations and irregular warfare at the lower end of the spectrum of conflict may improve opportunities to preempt development of viable insurgencies in the future.

COIN experiences of France in Algeria and the U.S. in Vietnam have demonstrated that operational success against insurgent forces late in a conflict may be negated by a loss of popular support at home. "It is a widely accepted truism that

France won the military battle in Algeria but lost the political war."[15] Early successes, especially if it were to preempt an insurgency, would be more palatable to the American people.

Proponents for focusing the Army on irregular warfare argue that its superior conventional capabilities will not be challenged any time soon. A focus on irregular warfare is prudent given the likelihood of commitment to irregular warfare. In testimony to the Senate Armed Services Committee, Andrew Krepinevich asserted "to be sure, our ground forces must remain dominate in conventional operations. However, it is far from clear that the Army and Marine Corps must be principally or even primarily devoted to this task." Potential adversaries such as Iran and North Korea have certainly taken note of America's supremacy in conventional capabilities and would thus focus on irregular warfare if faced with an open conflict with the United States.[16] They have seen the vulnerabilities of the United States to unconventional threats and the uncertain will of the American people in cases of protracted conflict.

The possibility of a major conventional war cannot be entirely discounted. Proponents for an irregular war focus contend that the sophistication of our equipment combined with our combined arms and joint capabilities are such an overmatch against potential adversaries that the Army can afford some degradation of its ability to fight a high intensity conflict. American forces would be capable of regaining conventional competence with a few months of training. Regardless, the Army would still be better prepared than its potential opponents for such an event. However, there may be some significant risk of taking this approach.

Israel's conflict in Lebanon against Hezbollah in 2006 is a relevant example of the risk of focusing on the lower end of the spectrum of conflict. The Israeli Defense Forces struggled during their offensive into southern Lebanon. They faced tough opposition from Hezbollah fighters in house to house urban combat with their Infantry forces, and their Armor units were severely disrupted by the intricate use of anti armor ambushes.[17]

Israeli ground units failed to dominate the battlefield with their conventional capabilities as would have been expected of an Army with their reputation. They were unprepared for a combined arms maneuver fight, in part because of their recent preoccupation as a constabalatory force. Their soldiers had spent most of their service manning checkpoints, patrolling, and conducting small raids against militants. They had not trained for major military actions as they felt the probability of such actions were remote.[18]

The early defeats of American forces in the Korea War, such as Task Force Smith, can be attributed to a lack of preparation of leaders and soldiers for major combat operations. An Army that just a few years earlier was the best in the world, suffered operational defeat against the Korean Army early in the conflict. The Post-World War II Army had been committed to occupation duties and had become essentially a constablatory force. The failure to prepare for major combat operations led to a force that was not motivated, equipped or trained to fight at the high end of the spectrum of conflict.[19]

Regain Focus for Major Combat Operations

Failure in general war or major combat operations is not an option. It is difficult to anticipate future threats and it takes time to build competency in conventional warfighting. It took almost 20 years to establish the competence that was demonstrated during the First Gulf War. It is not feasible to quickly "spin up" units, especially if they lack experienced leaders. China, Russia, North Korea, and other nations have significant conventional forces that could threaten our security in the future.

The Army has been fighting the Global War on terror for over seven years. The result is a company grade officer corps and junior NCO cadre with training, education, and combat experience that is overwhelmingly COIN centric. Many officers and NCOs have never experienced conventional combined arms operations either in training or in combat. Most of their institutional training has also been focused on COIN rather than learning about major combat operations. In a couple of years, the Army will have an entire cadre of battalion commanders whose entire field-grade experiences have been focused on combating insurgencies in Iraq and Afghanistan. These future commanders have never synchronized maneuver, fire, and logistics for a combined arms fight over extended battlespace in training or in combat.[20]

It took an intensive investment over several decades for the Army to gain its preeminence in combined arms and joint competencies in major combat operations. Demands of the Global War on Terror resulted in an absence of the very training and education programs that allowed the Army to prevail in Desert Storm and the initial stages of Iraqi Freedom. Defeat in a major combat operation would likely be much more damaging to America's security than failure in a counterinsurgency campaign. This is particularly true if casualties and equipment losses of a magnitude not seen since the Korean or Vietnam War were to occur. The damage to America's ability to exert national power in support of its interests could be significantly challenged if it was unsuccessful in a major conventional operation. Defeat in an irregular campaign is costly as well, but the Army is now well-grounded in stability and COIN, and those competencies will be resident in our force for the next two decades.

The Army's ranks are filled with leaders experienced in COIN and stability operations, many with multiple tours in Iraq and Afghanistan. It can be argued that these leaders will ensure that the officer and NCO corps retain expertise in counterinsurgency operations and possess the competencies to educate and train future leaders and soldiers should the Army be committed to combating future insurgencies.

While the risk of losing a major conventional war is potentially catastrophic, many would criticize a return to pre-9-11 focus on conventional warfighting. The United States has clearly demonstrated its awesome conventional warfighting capabilities to the international community. Potential adversaries are unlikely to expend their nation's resources to build a conventional capability that threatens to match America's military. Andrew Krepinevich stated "given the overwhelming success of our ground forces in conventional warfare operations, and the shift of rival militaries and non-state entities toward irregular warfare, orienting 48 active Army brigades, 28 National Guard brigades, and three Marine Corps divisions primarily on conventional warfare operations would appear to reflect a desire to prepare for the kinds of challenges we would prefer to confront, rather than those we will most likely encounter."[21]

Maintaining proficiency for counterinsurgency would be another concern if the Army was to refocus on conventional warfighting. While the Army possesses an experienced force now, this experience will begin to diminish over time. Many leaders are leaving the Army and taking their knowledge with them. Additionally, our veterans will become senior leaders in a few years and lose some of their ability to personally influence junior leaders and soldiers conducting stability operations and counterinsurgency in the future. The Army is well aware of the strategic impact made by soldiers at the lowest levels. Counterinsurgency skills will atrophy over time if not adequately addressed in officer and NCO professional education programs and training programs.

Organize Specialized Units

One course of action that has been suggested for the Army for optimizing the Army for full-spectrum capabilities is by organizing specialized units. These specialized units would create "expert" capabilities within the Army to maintain a mix of resident competencies available for commitment to various contingencies. The creation of a constablatory force similar to the Italian carabinieri that could be employed in stability operations is one example.[22] Currently, the Army lacks the luxury of maintaining forces that can provide expert capabilities across the range of requirements.

Recently the Army's Special Forces (Green Berets) were America's counterinsurgency force capable of conducting COIN training and serving as advisors. They are also capable of conducting direct action missions to kill or capture high-value targets.[23] Operations in Iraq and Afghanistan clearly demonstrated that American Special Forces lack the capacity to support operations on the scale found in Iraq. The

Army could reorganize or refocus its training and education programs to build expert capabilities throughout the force to mitigate the shortcomings of the Army in counterinsurgency, stability, and conventional warfighting.

Steven Metz and Frank Hoffman offer a proposal according to which ground forces could organize into three types of forces: conventional warfighting, counterinsurgency and stabilization, and homeland defense. This proposal entails a warfighting component that would be comprised of conventional mechanized and armor units supported by conventional support units such as field artillery and attack aviation. The Army would also have a component focused on counterinsurgency and stability operations. These units would have unique training requirements including language, culture, and governance. These units would be able to fill the gap for civilian capacity when necessary by addressing the problems of law enforcement and infrastructure repair. [24]

Another proposal is to redesign Maneuver Enhancement Brigades with the capability to fulfill stability functions to support the warfighting brigades. Bryan Watson offers that "the Army should immediately designate the Maneuver Enhancement Brigade as the primary support brigade responsible for providing a capability to handle stabilization efforts at the tactical level". These specialized units would be capable of accepting a "battle handover" of stabilization from the brigade combat teams allowing them to focus on decisive operations. This course of action would require them to possess the capability to serve as a warfighting headquarters and handle stability operations.[25]

Numerous arguments exist that oppose developing specialized units to handle specific functions within the spectrum of conflict. Concerns include a lack of depth to handle future conflicts which could exist at either end of the spectrum. Operation Iraqi Freedom and Enduring Freedom have stretched the force very thin. Specialized units would be committed to operations outside the scope of their specialties if similar force levels were required. This raises some serious questions concerning the effectiveness of this kind of strategy. How effective would counterinsurgent forces be if committed to a major conventional operation? What would happen if a stability force, like that proposed for Enhancement Brigades, was confronted by a formidable insurgent force? Finally, how long would it take conventional forces to adapt to stability and counterinsurgency operations once conventional operations are officially terminated?

Steven Metz and Raymond Miller argue that the Army should not develop specialized units for counterinsurgency operations. Their argument is that counterinsurgency should only be viewed as an "emergency expedient, undertaken only when necessary for the shortest period of time possible." Therefore investment of specialized forces would not be a prudent use of the nation's resources. Their view is that tactical skills needed for counterinsurgency would be close enough to that already resident in the force that units would be able to adapt through training.[26]

Michael O'Hannon provides another argument against developing specialized units. He discusses the risk that in peace operations it may be necessary to renew conflict or to fight a counterinsurgency. Combat units are trained to win and can inspire respect and fear from those who challenge them. He agrees that the requirements of operations similar to Iraq, Afghanistan, and even the initial operations in Bosnia exceed the capabilities of specialized units.[27]

Lieutenant General Chiarelli argues that that the Army should not reorganize into specialized units. His concerns are that the concept is "both unsustainable and unaffordable" and that "we simply don't have the resources to divide the military into "combat" and "stability" organizations. Instead, we must focus on developing full-spectrum capabilities across all organizations in the armed forces."[28]

Accept a Balance in COIN and Major

> One of the biggest challenges the Army faces, is to regain its traditional edge at fighting conventional wars while retaining what it has learned – and unlearned – about unconventional wars, the ones most likely to be fought in the years ahead.[29]

The Army has habitually focused its efforts toward the preparation for major combat operations at the higher end of the spectrum unless overly committed to operations at the lower end of the spectrum i.e. Post World War II occupation duties, Vietnam, and the current operations in Iraq and Afghanistan. The transition from preparing for operations at one end of the spectrum to its diametric opposite, leaving behind what was emphasized over years of education and training, is a time consuming process. It is a process that will require the Army's leaders to learn while in the crucible of combat. This is less than ideal as history has repeatedly demonstrated.

William L. Nash the Director of the Military Fellows Program testified before the House Armed Services Committee that "A general purpose force, trained, prepared, and equipped for high-intensity combat and stabilization and reconstruction is best suited to navigate the gray-zone between conflict and post-conflict operations."[30] The Army's doctrine and national policy demands a force ready to conduct offense, defense, and stability operations throughout the full spectrum of conflict. Given the nature of conflict over the past decade, units may have little time to adapt training toward a specific type of conflict. Further, proficiency is gained through sustained training and education programs. Leaders cannot simply "cram" to mitigate their ignorance in a form of conflict they are not prepared to conduct.

Leaders must be prepared to execute any type of military operation with little time to prepare. Lieutenant General Chiarelli advises that military forces must accept that decisive power may not be kinetic. The military must be able to remain competent in defeating enemies with traditional capabilities while offering hope to populations affected by war that its presence will improve their prospects in the future.[31] We do not have the luxury to pick which wars we will fight in the future. This exacerbates the challenge of predicting the type and nature of the conflicts in which we may become committed.

While campaigning for the presidency in 2000 Governor George W. Bush of Texas was quoted as saying "I mean, we're going to have kind of a nation building corps from America? Absolutely not. Our military is meant to fight and win war." That same year during a campaign stop, he stated "I'm worried about an opponent who uses nation building and the military in the same sentence."[32] How far out was the end of the cold war predicted? Most American military officers in the late 1980's envisioned a career focused on containing communism around the world and preparing for a possible war with the Soviet Union. This inability to predict future threats and the uncertainly of decisions that will be made by America's politically leaders does not allow the military to

18

accurately anticipate a particular form of conflict to which it may be committed in the near or distant future.

Adoption of a balanced approach to prepare the Army for full spectrum operations has its own critics. Time is one critical factor that challenges a balance of education and training for full spectrum operations. There will be a cost if the Army chooses to balance requirements for educating and training leaders in the diverse competencies required for conventional and irregular warfare, offense, defense, and stability operations. This cost is less than optimal competence across the full spectrum operations that our forces may find themselves facing in the future. It has been stated that "ground forces could easily become a jack-of-all-trades and master of none". Thus the potential for initial failure may be greater than any of the other approaches since the force is sub optimized for an effective response in any given mission"[33]

Another critique of a balanced approach is the ability of leaders and their soldiers to handle the diverse skill and knowledge needed to have competence in the full range of possible operations. A balanced training and education program would increase demands on leaders by expanding their competencies beyond that required by focusing on a specific skill set. Prior to current operations in Iraq and Afghanistan, leaders and soldiers focused on conventional operations and were extremely competent in this area. Now leaders are competent in counterinsurgency as a result of significant changes to education and training programs, and the operational experience gained through multiple deployments.

It can be argued that the Army's long term outlook is dismal with an under strength officer corps with automatic promotions into leadership positions along with a high demand for non-commissioned officers to attend Officer Candidate School. The stresses of the personnel system coupled with a requirement for everyone to achieve competence in full-spectrum operation may surpass the capabilities of the Army's leaders.[34]

Conclusion

> Military forces must prepare for the wars they may have to fight, not for the wars they want to fight. They must also prepare knowing that nothing about the history of warfare indicates that peacetime planners can count on predicting when a war takes place or how it will unfold.[35]

There are potentially serious implications with COIN centric training over several years with no immediate end in sight. Leaders and their soldiers are gaining competency in their ability to conduct counterinsurgency; however, they are losing their edge to conduct major conventional combat operations. We cannot rest on the conventional successes we've enjoyed during the initial stages of operations in Afghanistan and Iraq. There are some relevant historical examples that should cause us concern. A balanced approach to education and training is clearly the answer.

Despite its inherent limitations discussed earlier, a balanced approach would best meet the needs of the Army in preparation for an uncertain future. Adoption of this approach requires the Army to accept a degree of degradation in its leader's competence in a particular form of conflict. A balanced training and education program would limit leaders from obtaining expertise in a particular area within the spectrum of conflict. However, the recommended approach best prepares the Army's leaders for the uncertainly of future conflict across the continuum of conflict by providing them with a solid base from which to adapt to a myriad of challenges they may face in the future.

A balanced approach ensures that the Army's leaders are exposed to operational concepts applicable throughout the spectrum of conflict. There are strong opinions that predict that future adversaries of the United States will continue to seek asymmetrical approaches to mitigate American conventional advantages, and irregular warfare is clearly a likely-hood for the Army in the future. These opinions do not preclude the possibility of a major conventional war, or even more likely, conflicts where adversaries employ a synergetic combination of conventional and irregular capabilities. This type of scenario has already been played out between Hezbollah and the Israeli Defense Forces.

The Army's leaders cannot accurately predict the nature of future military commitments with any certainly. Focusing exclusively on irregular warfare or conventional war based on operational experiences both resident in the force today would be a mistake. Professional competencies are perishable over time as knowledge gained from experience decays over time and are also lost due to the effects of routine personnel turnover. The Army's training centers have demonstrated the degradation of training readiness demonstrated by comparing proficiency at the start and end of a training rotation. Routine personal turnover due to end tour of service (ETS) and retirements result in a significant loss of operational experiences over time. Leaders and their units will struggle in the future should they be committed to a conflict significantly different from what it had been training and educated to accomplish.

A balanced approach has the potential to develop leaders best postured to quickly adapt during an imminent crisis. Leaders would have training, educational, and perhaps operational experiences that would enable them to quickly prepare for both conventional and irregular contingencies. This course of action is clearly preferable to the drastic measures taken to develop counterinsurgency competence as we began stability operations in a counterinsurgency environment in Iraq and Afghanistan.

Endnotes

[1] General Jack Keane, *Jim Lehrer News Hour*, 18 April 2006; quoted in U.S. Department of the Army and U.S. Marine Corps, *The U.S. Army - Marine Corps Counterinsurgency Field Manual*, Army Field Manual 3-24, Marine Corps Warfighting Publication 3-33.5 (Chicago: University of Chicago Press, 2007), xiv.

[2] David Galula, *Counterinsurgency Warfare: Theory and Practice* (New York: Praeger, 1964), 88-89.

[3] Andrew Feickert, *Does the Army Need a Full-Spectrum Force or Specialized Units?* (Washington, D.C.: Library of Congress, Congressional Research Service, 18 January 2008), 6.; and Jack D. Crabtree III, Small Group Instructor, United States Army Infantry School, email message to author, 4 January 2008.

[4] Claude W. Bowman, Chief of Academic Operations U.S. Army Command and General Staff College, email message to author, 7 January 2008.

[5] Feickert, 6.

[6] BG Robert W. Cone, "The Changing National Training Center," *Military Review* 86 (May-June 2006): 71-73.

[7] Ibid., 73-74.

[8] Ibid., 75.

[9] James B. Mingo, Senior Trainer, Operations Group, National Training Center, e-mail message to author, 25 February 2008.

[10] Oscar F. Diano, *The Combat Training Centers: Training for Full-Spectrum Operations?*, Masters Thesis (Fort Leavenworth, KS: U.S. Command and General Staff College, 2007), 5-6.

[11] John M. Donnelly, "Small Wars, Big Changes," *CQ Weekly* (28 January 2008): 252 ; [journal on-line]; available from http://public.cq.com/docs/cqw/weeklyreport110-000002661193.html; Internet; accessed 19 March 2008.

[12] Ibid.

[13] Andrew F. Krepinevich, *The Future of U.S. Ground Forces: Challenges and Requirements*, Testimony (Washington, D.C.: Center for Strategic and Budgetary Assessments, 17 April 2007), 5 ; available from http://www.csbaonline.org/4Publications/PubLibrary/T.20070417.The_Future_of_US_G/T.20070417.The_Future_of_US_G.pdf; Internet; accessed 1 January 2008.

[14] Ibid.

[15] Peter Chalk, "Algeria: 1954-1962," in Angel Rabasa, et al., *Money in the Bank: Lessons Learned from Past Counterinsurgency (COIN) Operations* (Santa Monica, CA: RAND, 2007), 25.

[16] Krepinevich, 9

[17] Institute for Strategic Studies, "Middle East/Gulf," in *Strategic Survey 2007* (London, England: Institute for Strategic Studies, 2007), 230 ; [database on-line]; available from InformaWorld; Internet; accessed 11 February 2008.

[18] Ibid.

[19] T.R. Fehrenbach, *This Kind of War* (New York: Macmillan Company, 1963). Author derived conclusions from study of book above.

[20] Diano, 6.

[21] Krepinevich, 10.

[22] Micheal O'Hannon, "The Need to Increase the Size of the Deployable Army," *Parameters* 34 (Autumn 2004): 7.

[23] Feickert, 11

[24] Ibid.

[25] Bryan Watson, *Reshaping the Expeditionary Army to Win Decisively: The Case for Greater Stabilization Capacity in the Modular Force* (Carlisle Barracks, PA: U.S. Army War College, Strategic Studies Institute, August 2005), 20 ; available from www.strategicstudiesinstitute.army.mil/pdffiles/pub621.pdf; Internet; accessed 2 February 2008.

[26] Steven Metz and Raymond Millen, *Insurgency and Counterinsurgency in the 21st Century: Reconceptionalizing Threat and Response* (Carlisle Barracks, PA: U.S. Army War College, Strategic Studies Institute, November 2004), 32.

[27] O'Hannon, 7.

[28] Peter W. Chiarelli, "Learning From Our Modern Wars: The Imperatives Of Preparing For A Dangerous Future," *Military Review* 87 (September – October 2007): 6.

[29] Donnelly, 252. Quote attributed to Secretary Robert M. Gates.

[30] William L. Nash, "Testimony: U.S. Post-Conflict Operations: Preparing our Military for the Future," 9 November 2005; available from http://www.cfr.org/publication/9210/us_postconflict_operations.html; Internet; accessed 9 March 2008.

[31] Chiarelli, 5.

[32] Donnelly, 252.

[33] Steven Metz and Frank Hoffman, *Restructuring America's Ground Forces: Better, Not Bigger*, Policy Analysis Brief (Muscatine, IA: Stanley Foundation, September 2007), 10 ; available from http://www.stanleyfoundation.org/publications/pab/Metz_HoffmanPAB07.pdf; Internet; accessed 9 March 2008.

[34] Feickert, 18

[35] Anthony H. Cordesman, *Preliminary "Lessons" of the Israeli-Hezbollah War* (Washington, D.C.: Center for Strategic and International Studies, Revised 17 August 2006), 23 ; available from http://www.csis.org/media/csis/pubs/060817_isr_hez_lessons.pdf; Internet; accessed 20 March 2008.